The Emancipated Kitchen

Many thanks
Mrs Hander,
with love
Marianne ♥

Marianna Cappelletti

The Emancipated Kitchen

TravellingBreeze Publishing

First edition 2015

The Emancipated Kitchen
by Marianna Cappelletti

ISBN 978-0-9932279-0-5

Published by
TravellingBreeze Publishing
London
travellingbreezepublishing@gmail.com
www.travellingbreezepublishing.com

Thanks Ada Valanzano, mum, for being a living inspiration of cooking passion and dedication.
Thanks Luigi & Mauro for all the creative, positive vibes and empathetic support.
Thank you Eva Maria & Viola, treasures of my life, precious Em Kitchen helpers, good food appreciators and blooming taste creatives.
Thank you.

Contents

Millet Tabbouleh 79
Millet Croccantina with Hot Chillie Beans 80
Chickpeas Focaccia 82
Oltrecielo, New Moon/Solar Eclipse Spicy
Cauliflower Pie 84
Em Burgers 87
Tofu, Aglio, Olio e Peperoncino Rice Linguine
89
Spaghetti with Beauty Spell Pesto 91
Spelt Pasta with Romanesco Broccoli and
Seitan of the LaboratorioVeg 93
Pumpkin, Olives and Seitan Penne 95
Em Ragu' Sauce with Seitan and Porcini
Mushrooms 96
Wholemeal Lasagna with Pumpkin and
Walnuts Sauce 98
Pasta with Courgettes 100
Creamy Curry with Pan Fried Koyadofu Cakes
101
Chickpeas Tagine 104
Seitan with Creamy Chickpeas Sauce of the
LaboratorioVeg 106
Seitan with Onions 108
Roast Potatoes or Pumpkin with Seitan 109
Lemon Soy Scaloppine 110
Em polenta 111
Quinoa Gnocchi with Radicchio and Walnut
Sauce 112

Occupy your kitchen!

Dear readers,

This is a collection of some of my personal recipes. They are what I normally eat. Natural, healthy and very tasteful recipes. I'm an Italian based in London yoga teacher, bohoyogini, food activist, blogger and other things. Passionate in finding and enjoying conscious paths in preparing and tasting emancipated and sensuous dishes, yes! Oh yes, they can go together, they must go together.

It's all about making choices, conscious, respectful, balance directed and coming from love choices: Emancipated (Em) choices. The kitchen as a creative laboratory for alchemies, good vibes and taste. And actually for some wild Shakti dancing!

The recipes are often for 4 people, but I encourage you to make the same quantity even if you are two or even one. I'm a big fan of left overs! Quick, easy, comforting, healthy and so worthy! Finding tempting, healthy and ready to eat food in the fridge is a clever trick to not choose the wrong snack or meal. Don't be discouraged if you're not vegetarian or vegan, I don't think that the answer is and has ever been in absolutism or self prohibition. Just try to introduce one, two, maybe more of animal free, emancipated days in your week and it will make a huge difference on you and on the planet.

So don't force yourself unkindly, make conscious decisions, little steps forward, and things will change on their own, at the right pace and time, your time. Start from the only place that can bring you the best results: enjoyment!

The recipes are grouped in 4 chapters.

Morning Inspirations. Which are some nice and wise ideas to inspire you for a sparkling super start.

Dips and Pates. As you will see some of them, if you dip in them bread or roasted potatoes chips for example, are proper mini meals themselves or very well balance little snacks. Others will be sexy company for whatever you like.

Mini Meals. They are always very well organized in terms of nutrients distribution, but they take up less time and effort to prepare them.

Main Meals and Celebration Recipes. Are well balanced dishes in terms of distribution of nutrients, very comforting and they can be considered for a principal meal or perfect for convivial ones.

Sweet Comforts and Raw Treats. Guess what? Sweet time! Proper delicious, healthy cakes and raw bites to treat you and your friend for dessert or tea time, or late night work snack time or late night sexy snack time.

The ingredients! Yes the ingredients! The quality is significant. I encourage to choose biodynamic (Demeter) when it is possible, but anyway, stay organic and as local and small as possible, when is possible.

Use only natural sea salt. As you will see I adore tamari and miso, try! Play with them, experiment with them. They are precious ingredients in terms of taste and health.

Sweeteners...You won't find sugar here. Exceptions are exceptions but do a favor to yourself and to the world and just don't buy it anymore.

I normally use agave syrup, but when we are making large puddings or cakes, I go for fructose, which is still a quite refined sweetener, but it helps to keep the GI of the recipe down and after all, we don't eat luxurious chocolate cakes every evening. Fats? Organic and cold pressed.

Got your shopping bag? Pour yourself a glass of wine (in wise quantity a great source of antioxidants and pleasure!). Don't forget the music and let's start making magic!

www.emkitchen.com
Like Em Kitchen on Facebook
Follow on Instagram @travellingbreeze
Follow on Twitter @Em Kitchen

With love and good intention,

Marianna ♥

Morning Inspirations

"Creativity is the greatest rebellion in existence." Osho

Start Day Tips

It is well known, a glass of warm water with lemon juice, first thing in the morning on an empty stomach is extremely good for you. It is a great start for so many healthy reasons first of all it is a superior body alkalizer.

Another good ancient alkaline remedy, coming from macrobiotics, is ½ teaspoon of umeboshi puree dissolved in some warm water.

If you do your yoga practice early in the morning, try a shot of matcha instead, before starting your practice.

To accompany your breakfast every kind of pure green teas are a treat.

If you drink coffee, try to contain the use of it. Vegetarian milks are all fine if organic.

Pure coconut water is a great drink during physical exercise.

A great drink choice are all fermented drinks like water and milk kefir and absolute my favorite, kombucha; my beloved treat after a yoga practice, actually just so perfect after yoga. It tastes so nice and the benefits are countless; because it is another powerful alkalizer, try to drink it on an empty stomach.

Two favorite Em Smoothies

Very easy goodness. Bleeeeeend!...And serve

Avocado Delight

1 avocado
1 banana
Juice of 2 lemons
Your favorite milk (or half veg milk/half water)
Agave or rice syrup to taste

Matcha Spell

1 slice of fresh pinapple
1 medium/small avocado
Juice of 1 lemon
Your favorite vegetarian milk (or half veg
milk/half water)
Agave syrup to taste
1 teaspoon of matcha

Quick Dates Jam

Ingredients

250g of pitted dried dates (better if quite soft)
Lemon and orange zest
Water

In the mixer, blend dates and zest using enough water to obtain a smooth jam consistency. Put the mixture in a clean glass jar with hermetic lid and keep it in the fridge. Taste it as a jam on toast, alone or with an healthy butter like almond, peanut or other.

* You can also try to substitute the dried dates with prunes or figs.

Em Crepes

Ingredients

120g of wholemeal flour (Wheat or Spelt)
250ml of almond milk
Sunflower, coconut or peanut oil
1 pinch of salt

Add the flour in a bowl, slowly pour the almond milk, the pinch of salt and mix well with a whisk until the mixture is smooth and fluid. Let it rest half an hour.
Grease a non-stick pan and pour a few tablespoons of the mixture. Cook on one side. As soon as the edges of the crepe curl, turn and finish cooking.
Continue until you finish the batter and place the crepes on a cutting board and fill them sweet or savory as you wish.

Matcha Cookies

Ingredients

100g of almond flour
80g of fructose
30g of good quality sunflower or corn germs or peanut oil
30g soy milk
1 teaspoon of matcha

Mix all the ingredient nicely together ad add the matcha at the end.
Place a sheet of baking paper on a tray. Drop full teaspoon of the matcha mixture gently on the baking paper living good space one from the other. In fact in the oven the mixture will melt down and make lovely round shape cookies, but they need space to not attach one to the other. Cook in a preheated oven at 180 degrees for about 12 minutes or until they start to golden. Don' t wait too much, otherwise they will golden too much and you will loose that bright green colour.
Let completely cool down before tasting.

Dates and Walnuts Muffins

Ingredients

200g of wholemeal spelt flour
100g of fructose
60g of roughly and finely crumbled walnuts
200g of pitted soft dates
200ml of soy milk
1/2 teaspoon of baking soda
Vanilla optional

Preheat the oven at 180 degrees.
Chop the dates finely, you can use the mixer.
In a bowl combine all the ingredients except
walnuts and dates. When the mixture is nice
and smooth add dates and walnuts and fill 2/3
of some nice paper muffin cases with it.
Sprinkle the top of each of them with a little of
extra fructose.
Cook in the oven for about 20 minutes and let
rest for about 10 minutes before eating.

Orange Muffins

Ingredients

150g of wholemeal spelt flour
100g of agave syrup
200g of pitted soft dates
100g of almond flour
150ml of almond milk
The juice of 1 orange
The zest of 1 orange
½ teaspoon of baking soda
2 tablespoon of a good quality and mild oil
100ml of water

Preheat the oven at 180 degrees.
Pure' the dates in the mixer with the water and combine the dates pure' with the rest of the ingredients, adding some extra almond milk if the mixture is too dry (this will depend on the softness of the dates).
When the mixture is nice and smooth, fill 2/3 of some paper muffin cases with it.
Cook in the oven for about 20 minutes and let rest for about 10 minutes before eating.

Chocolate Cookies

Ingredients

100g of almond flour
100g of plain flour
100 gr of fructose
200ml of almond milk
50 gr of cocoa powder
½ teaspoon of baking soda

Mix well all the ingredients until the mixture is nice and smooth.
Place a sheet of baking paper on a baking tray and gently place a spoon of the mixture on it, repeat until you finish it. With the help of a spoon, shape and flatten your cookies a little bit, and bake them in preheated oven at 180 degrees for about 15 minutes.

Peanuts Cookies

Ingredients

200g of white flour (or 50% white and 50% wholemeal)
100g of fructose
100ml of soy milk
2 tablespoons of peanut butter
1/3 of a teaspoon of cinnamon
150gr of peanut
¼ of a teaspoon of salt

Mix all the ingredients, except the peanuts, until you have a nice and smooth mixture. Add the peanuts and mix well.
Place a sheet of baking paper on a baking tray and adjust tablespoons of the mixture on it, and with the help of a spoon, shape them like nice flat cookies and bake in preheated oven at 180 degrees, for about 15 minutes, until golden brown.

Dips & Pates

"Music gives a soul to the universe, wings to the mind, flight to the imagination and life to everything." Plato

Tamari Seasoning

Ingredients

2 full teaspoons of barley or rice miso paste
2 tablespoons of water
150ml of tamari
The juice of 1 lemon
2 teaspoons of agave syrup
1 pinch of chili powder

Dissolve the miso paste with a couple of tablespoons of water, maybe more depending on the consistency of your miso, until nice and soupy.
Add the lemon juice, the agave syrup, the tamari and the chili powder and stir well. Pour in a glass soy sauce bottle, shake well and use like you normally use your tamari sauce, rice, noodles, stir fries, marinades etc. You're going to be addicted to this!

Watercress Miso Dressing

Ingredients

100g of watercress
50ml of apple vinegar
2 teaspoons of agave syrup
100ml of extra virgin olive oil
2 teaspoons of white miso paste
Salt and pepper to taste

Blend all the ingredients, until you have a nice and fluid consistency. It is ready. It goes really well with steamed vegetables, new potatoes, sweet potatoes, fine beans, carrots, broccoli, asparagus, etc.

Mustard Miso Salad Dressing

Ingredients

1 teaspoon of miso paste
1 teaspoon of Dijon mustard
1 tablespoon of agave syrup
2 teaspoons of apple vinegar
1 pinch of black pepper
25ml of extra virgin olive oil

Dissolve the miso paste in a little water. Add all the rest of the ingredients, mix well and use to dress your favorite salad.

Miso Dip

Ingredients

3 teaspoons of rice or barley miso paste
1 full tablespoon of extra virgin olive oil
1 teaspoon of pumpkin seeds oil
1 pinch of cumin
1 pinch of thyme
1 pinch of chili powder
1 teaspoon of lemon juice or balsamic vinegar
Water

Dissolve the miso paste with a little bit of water. Add all the other ingredients and mix well.
It s sublime with home made still warm bread or boiled new potatoes.
With this easy dip you can play to experiment and enjoy all the goodness and properties of different kinds of good cold pressed organic oils, like oil of walnut, wheat germs and many more.

Miso & Tahini Dip

Ingredients

1 tablespoon of white miso paste
1 tablespoon of tahini
The juice of 1 lemon
Water

Mix together the miso paste and tahini adding the lemon juice first and then enough water to obtain a smooth, creamy consistency. Done!
Try with tempura or roasted chips. And of course falafel!

*You could use other kinds of miso, like dark rice or barley ones. In this case add ½ tablespoon of agave syrup to the ingredients.

Ginger Miso Dip

Ingredients

3 teaspoons of white miso paste
Shoyu
1 teaspoon of sesame seeds or a finely
chopped spring onion
Ginger

Dissolve the miso paste with enough water to obtain a smooth, creamy consistency. Add two or three tablespoons of shoyu, the sesame seeds or the spring onion and grated ginger to taste. Delicious with tempura, pan fried tofu, mochi* rice cakes wrapped in nori, and roast vegetables.

*You can make your mochi frying it with a little oil at low heat and with the lid on, until it puffs like popcorn and turns golden on each side. Wrap it in a piece of toasted nori and dip in your favorite seasoning. Thank you Japan!

Em Mayo

Ingredients

100ml almond or soy milk
150ml circa of a mild oil like corn germs oil,
sunflower or soy oil.
50ml circa of extra virgin olive oil
Salt
Juice of 1 lemon
Dijon mustard (optional)
Saffron

Put the milk in the mixer and blend it for few
seconds until nice and velvety. Start adding
the oil very slowly while you keep blending.
The amount of oil you will need is
approximate, so make sure you stop adding it
to the milk just when you reach the right mayo
consistency. And consider also that once in
the fridge, your Em Mayo will thicken more if
you used soy milk. At this point add the olive
oil and then salt, lemon juice, saffron and
mustard to taste. Remember to taste it while
you're adding the flavoring ingredients. They

really depends on your taste. This mayo is a blessing! And don't be afraid to try to make it, it is really that easy!

Miso Em Mayo
Instead of salt add 2 teaspoons of miso paste. My favorite!

Wasabi Em Mayo
Instead of saffron and mustard, add wasabi to taste.

Em Aoli
Blend in 3 cloves of garlic at the end.

*Once you've learned to make the classic Em Mayo you can experiment adding other ingredients like parsley, chillies, tarragon etc.

Aubergine Miso Pate'

Ingredients

2 aubergines
2 tablespoons of Miso Em Mayo (p. 38)
2 tablespoons of tahini
3 garlic cloves
½ teaspoon of cumin
3 tablespoons of lemon juice
Extra virgin olive oil
More miso paste to taste if required

Put the whole aubergines in a preheated oven and cook until soft.
Remove the skin and place the flesh in a container. Add the tahini, crushed garlic, cumin, lemon juice, the Em Miso Mayo and mash well with a fork. Don't use the blender, otherwise you will loose that nice aubergine texture. Taste and decide if you need to add a little bit of miso to make the pate' more savory. In this case dissolve a little bit of miso paste with a little water and add to the pate'. Stir in a couple of tablespoons of olive oil at the end.

Stir Fry Paste

Ingredients

70g of peanuts
30ml extra virgin olive oil
10ml sesame oil
3 cloves of garlic
3 tablespoons of tamari
2 teaspoons of white miso paste
1 teaspoon of gave syrup

In the mixer blend all the ingredients except miso.
Dissolve the miso with a little water until creamy and smooth and add to the rest. Use as a paste for every stir fry, noodles, rice, vegetables.
You can add it at the end. Just mix your dish a couple of time more on the heat before serving.

Yogurt Dip

Ingredients

150g of soy yogurt
1 red onion
1 clove of garlic
1 bunch of parsley
1 or 2 deseeded red chillies
Salt to taste

Blend all the ingredients and enjoy! Lovely with falafel and all kinds of tempura.

*If you like you can try adding ½ deseeded cucumber to the ingredients.

Funky Diva Beets Dip

Ingredients

250 gr of boiled beetroots
100 gr of cooked chickpeas
2 tablespoons of Em Mayo (p. 37)
3 spring onions
3 juniper berries
1 teaspoon of a good dijon mustard
Pepper
Salt to taste
Blend all the ingredients! Le jeu sont fait!

Toasted rye bread, wholemeal focaccia, chips, savory pancakes of all kinds. Easy funky matching!

*Instead of the 2 tablespoons of Em Mayo you could also try adding 3 full tablespoons of hummus.

Kali's Dip

Ingredients

3 red peppers
2 onions
3 cloves of garlic
2 teaspoons of paprika
1 tablespoon of white miso paste
Hot chili powder to taste

Cut peppers, onions and garlic. Put them in a boiling pan with two tablespoons of water, cover with lid and let cook until they soft. Add the paprika and cook for another minute. Transfer everything in a bowl and let cool down. Once cool, blend adding the miso paste and enough chili powder to make it hot, otherwise it can't be called Kali's dip, and I can't tell you exactly how much chili powder you need because the powders can be very different one from another, so taste. Let rest the dip in the fridge for an hour at least.
Try with some lovely crispy potatoes, sliced like crisps and roasted with the skin on.

Em Ketchup

Ingredients

700ml of tomato passata
2 tablespoons of tomato concentrate
130g of celery
1 carrot
1 onion
1 little piece of ginger
3 cloves of garlic
1 pinch of rosemary
1 pinch of black pepper
5 cloves
30ml of apple vinegar
1 teaspoon of salt
1 full tablespoon of fructose
2 teaspoons of miso paste

Put all the ingredients in a pan except the miso, vinegar and fructose. Add a glass of water and cook until all the vegetables are nice and soft.

Discard the ginger and the cloves and let it cool down.
Blend everything adding the vinegar, the fructose and the miso paste.
Fill some ketchup bottles and treat your inner child!
You can safely refrigerate it for a week.

Tomatoes and Kombu Salsa

Ingredients

1 sheet of kombu of about 10cm, soaked in
warm water for about 10 minutes
1 little bunch of coriander
1 little bunch of rocket
5 red medium tomatoes
100g of spring onions
2 fresh chillies, halved and deseeded
1 tablespoon of extra virgin olive oil
Tamari to taste

You could simply blend all the ingredients, it
will taste good but it will have a greeny browny
look, to avoid that, finely chop the coriander
and the rocket in the mixer and put it aside.
Now you can blend all the rest of the
ingredients and add the chopped coriander
and rocket at the end. Stir well and rest in the
fridge for at least 1 hour.

Green Hippie Dip

Ingredients

500g of spinach
250g of tofu
A bunch of spring onions
The juice of 1 lemon
2 teaspoons of miso paste
Tamari to taste
Extra virgin olive oil

Boil the spinach leaves and let them cool.
Blend together the tofu, spinach, lemon juice,
miso paste, tamari and a couple of
tablespoons of olive oil, until nice and smooth
(maybe you'll like to add a couple of
tablespoons of water too, it depends on the
tofu consistency). Add the spring onions and
blend for few other seconds. Ready! You are
going to be impressed! I tried it with some
quick home made Quick Grissini (p. 62), so
lovely!

Butter Beans and Chillies Pate'

Ingredients

250g cooked butter beans
4 cloves of garlic
1 tablespoon of white miso paste
1 bunch of parsley
The juice of 1 lemon
3 deseeded green chillies
3 tablespoon of extra virgin oil of olive

Finely chop the parsley and blend all the rest of the ingredients adding little drops of water until you've reached the right hummus consistency, sprinkle with the parsley and serve with focaccia bread, rustic organic crackers or with anything you like.

Cannellini and Mushrooms Pate'

Ingredients

250g of cooked cannellini beans
2 cloves of garlic
3 tablespoons of extra virgin oilive oil
300 gr of mushrooms
Salt and pepper

Sauté the cut mushrooms for about 15 minutes with the cloves of garlic, 2 tablespoons of oil of olive and enough salt and pepper to taste.
Blend the cannellini beans with the garlic mushrooms and a tablespoon of olive oil.
Taste the dip and add some salt if it needs it.
It is just perfect like this, but if you want to add some more character, you can stir in some drops of truffles oil to taste.
Just put all the ingredients in a blender and you're done!
Perfect to find in the fridge after your late evening yoga class. You can spread it over your favorite bread, focaccia or to fill a wrap.

Dhal Hummus

Ingredients

250g of dhal
600ml water
1 tablespoon of tahini
3 teaspoons of white miso paste
5 tablespoons of extra virgin olive oil
½ teaspoon of paprika
1 pinch of cumin
2 cloves of garlic
2 red chillies
Salt

Put everything in the mixer and blend until nice
and smooth. Adjust the salt and to serve put in
a nice ceramic bowl and add a little of olive oil
and paprika on top.

Mini Meals

"Everything in the universe is within you. Ask all from yourself."
Rumi

Spicy Cauliflower Frittelle with Yogurt Dip

Ingredients

1 cauliflower previously cut into small pieces
and steamed or boiled al dente
Chickpeas flour as needed
Water as required
1 teaspoon of curry powder
Sunflower oil

Mix in a bowl the chickpeas flour and water
and make a thick not liquid batter, enough for
all the cauliflower that you have. Let it rest in
the fridge for 10/30 minutes.
Dip the cauliflower pieces into the batter and
with the help of a spoon fry them in very hot
oil.
My frittelle felt in love for the yogurt dip (p. 41)
Enjoy! Actually the left overs are delicious
even cold for a happy snack.

Fried Not Fried Aubergines with Tahini Dip

Ingredients for the aubergine

1 medium aubergine
150g of wholemeal flour
1/2 teaspoon of baking soda
Extra virgin olive oil
Water

Ingredients for the dip

2 tablespoons of tahini
2 tablespoons of white miso paste
The juice of 1 lemon
Water

Slice the aubergine. Combine flour with the baking soda and slowly add water little by little until you have a smooth and thick batter. Place some oven paper on a tray and oil it. Dip nicely the slices of aubergine and arrange them on the tray. If you have some batter left

just pour it on the tray next to the aubergines, it will be a nice pancake. Spill some oil on top and straight in the oven at 200 degrees until nice golden and crisp.
While they are cooking you can make the dip. Dissolve the tahini with the lemon juice and the miso paste with a little of water, mix them together and if it's a little too thick keep dissolving the mixture with a little more water. All done!

Carrot Frittelle with
Sexy Red Hot Chilli Miso Dip

Ingredients for the frittelle

200g of carrots cut in little stripes or grated
250g of wholemeal flour
Sea salt
Corn, sunflower or peanut oil

Ingredients for the dip

3 medium red peppers
125g of white miso paste
2 cm ginger
2 tablespoons of sesame seeds
1 pinch of chilli pepper powder
1 teaspoon of tamari
1 teaspoon of sake' or rice wine

Remove the seeds from the peppers, wash
them, cut them in pieces of about 2 x 2 cm and
place them in a tray with only some sea salt.
Cook them at 220 degrees until they start

browning on the edges. Put them aside to cool.

Grate the carrots or cut them in tiny stripes. Mix 1/4 of teaspoon of sea salt with the flour and blend them with enough water to obtain a creamy butter.

Blend the cooked peppers with the tamari and sake (or rice wine) until it is completely creamy. Then grate the ginger in it and add the chilli powder, the sesame seeds and finally the miso paste. Mix really well with a spoon and keep it in the fridge.

Heat some corn or peanut oil in a large pan to fry the frittelle.

Add the carrots to the butter, mix well and place a spoon of this mixture in the very hot oil. Turn them few times until they are golden brown on both sides.

Serve them hot with the dip on the side.

(If you have any frittelle left they are lovely for breakfast with canadian marple syrup!)

Corn and Feta Frittelle

Ingredients

100g of wholemeal spelt flour
285g of cooked corn
100ml of water
200g of feta cheese
Salt
Extra virgin olive oil

To make the batter, just mix the spelt flour with the water, a pinch of salt and mix well until smooth. The batter should be quite thick.
Place a sheet of baking paper on a baking tray and spread it with a little olive oil.
Crumble the feta cheese in the batter and add the corn too. Mix gently and shape flat cakes on the baking paper. You wont be able to do it with your hands, use a spoon. Dash a little olive on top of each frittella and bake in preheated oven at 200 degrees until golden brown on both sides. You have to turn them a couple of time while they are cooking but don't do it too soon or they will break.

Dhal and Coconut Soup

Ingredients

2 carrots
1 onion
3 cloves of garlic
1 red chilli
1 medium potato
200g of dhal
Good quality curry masala
300g of basmati rice
125g of coconut cream

Roughly cut carrots, onion, chilli, garlic and potato, in a pan and cover with water, add the dhal, an organic vegetarian stock cube and bring to boil.
Let cook until the vegetables and dhal are nice and soft. Add a full tablespoon of curry masala and let cook for another 2 minutes. Add the coconut cream and stir for other two minutes.
Let everything cool for 15 minutes, in the meantime prepare your steam rice.
Rinse the rice under cold water until the water

runs clear.

Place rice in a medium saucepan and cover with water. The water should be 1 centimeter over the rice. Bring to a boil over high heat. Cover with lid and reduce heat to low. Simmer undisturbed until rice is tender, about 15 minutes. Remove from heat and let sit covered to steam, about 5 minutes.

With a blender purée the vegetables and dhal in the pan and add a little water if it is necessary to reach your ideal soup consistency.

Add the rice to the soup and tamari to taste. You can make quite a big pan of soup with the ingredients I suggested. But it is so good up to three days in the fridge and you can have a ready mini meal anytime, just warming it up a little.

*Instead of basmati rice you can serve the soup with some nice wholemeal bread or focaccia

Adzuki Bean Soda Bread

Ingredients

300g of wholemeal spelt flour
1/3 of teaspoon of baking soda
180ml of water
½ teaspoon of salt
200g of cooked adzuki beans
1 tablespoon of sesame seeds
1 tablespoon of flaxseeds powder (you can make them yourself just blend the flaxseeds in the mixer for few seconds)

Mix together all the ingredients except the adzuki beans. Make a nice and smooth dough. Add the adzuki beans and mix gently in the dough. The beans will mash a little, that is just as it should be.
Shape the dough as you like and bake in preheated oven at 180 degrees for about 40 minutes.

Quick Grissini Bread

Ingredients

225g wholemeal flour
1/4 teaspoon of baking soda
150 ml of water
1/2 teaspoon of salt
Nuts or seeds (optional)

Dissolve the yeast or baking soda and salt in a little of the water and then add to the rest of the water. If you are using nuts or seeds combine them with the flour and the water mix. Stir with a wooden spoon then knead with your hands.
Tip on to a lightly floured surface and knead until smooth but not sticky.
With your hand roll some kind of snakes of about 1-2 cm of diameter, don t measure them :-) By the way this is something nice to do even with kids, because they can mould by hands; they are easy, fast and fresh bread is always a treat!
You have your bread snakes, now bake them in a preheated oven at 200 degrees for about

10 minutes, until nice and golden.
What makes these grissini a mini meal is that you can enjoy them with one of the dips suggested and you will have something very tasteful and complete from a nutritional perspective, in a very short time.

* You can use any kind of flour. If you are eating them with a dip containing too little protein like the tomatoes and seaweed one, you could use 175g flour and 50g of soya flour or add some crumble nuts or seeds to the dough, so at the end you will have a good balanced mini meal.

Em Pizzette

Ingredients for the pizzette base

300g plain white flour
150g chickpeas flour
1 teaspoon of salt
½ teaspoon of bicarbonate of soda
1 tablespoon of extra virgin olive oil
Water

Mix oil and salt in the water and then add the rest of the water. Add the yeast. Stir with a wooden spoon, then knead with your hands. Let the dough rest for half an hour.
At this point, with the help of a rolling pin and without being too perfectionist, start making some little pizzas with a diameter of about 15 cm more or less. Place them on a baking tray, you can use some eco roasting paper underneath if you like and start to dress them.

With courgettes and walnut sauce
Cut a courgette in very thin slices.
Blend 200 gr of walnuts with a small garlic clove, a pinch of paprika, black pepper and enough soy milk to make a smooth and thick

sauce.

Arrange the courgette slices on the pizzette, put a little of salt and oil of olive on top. Cook in the oven at maximum heat for about 10 minutes. Take them out, distribute some walnut sauce on top and cook for about other 3 minutes or until the pizzettes have a lovely ready to be assaulted look.

With tomatoes, garlic and sesame seeds

Spread some canned chopped tomatoes or some tomato passata on top of the pizzette and a little salt and oil of olive on top. Cook in the oven at maximum heat for about 10 minutes.

In the meantime, crush 3 garlic cloves and mix them with some good quality olive oil.

Take the pizzette out of the oven and sprinkle some sesame seeds on top. Cook for about other 3 minutes and before serving add little drops of the garlic and oil mixture.

With potatoes, rosemary and black pepper

Slice some organic potatoes very thin, without peeling off the skin. Arrange the slices on the pizzette with some salt, pepper and olive oil. Let them cook at maximum heat for about ten minutes. Take them out of the oven and sprinkle some rosemary on top. Let cook for about other 3 minutes and serve.

*Lots of other vegetables work nice on the pizzette. Instead of the potatoes you could slice some red onions and crumble some fry scrambled tofu on top at the end. Or make the pizzette just plain and add some rocket, chopped red tomatoes, salt and some garlic oil.

Tofu and Carrots Kebabs

Ingredients

200g of tofu
5 carrots
Corn germs oil (or olive oil)
Tamari
Sesame seeds

Cut the carrots and put them in the oven with a little oil. Cut the tofu in cubes and put it in a bowl. When the carrots start to soften add them to the tofu and mix well everything with a bit of oil and 1 full tablespoon of tamari. Prepare the kebabs, alternating carrots pieces and tofu cubes. Put them in the oven until nice and crispy and sprinkle with sesame seeds for the last two or three minutes. Serve with vegan mayo on the side.

Seitan and Rocket Salad

Ingredients

150g of seitan
100g of rocket
150g of little cherry tomatoes chopped in half
1 handful of spring onions chopped
1 little raw beetroot finely chopped
Extra virgin olive oil
Umeboshi vinegar
Balsamic vinegar
Pepper
Tamari

Cut the seitan in cubes, dress it with a little of olive oil and 2 tablespoons of tamari, saute' for 5-7 minutes add and set aside.
In a bowl mix rocket, tomatoes and spring onions and dress with olive oil, balsamic vinegar, pepper, a touch of umeboshi vinegar and pepper. Add the seitan and mix well.

Tofu, Potatoes and Black Olives

Ingredients

500g of new potatoes
300g of tofu
150g of black olives
Tamari
Finely chopped fresh parsley
Extra virgin olive oil

Cut the new potatoes and roast them just with a bit of olive oil, don't put to much oil, use your hands to dress them nicely.
Dress the tofu with a bit of tamari, oil and pan fry it in a large non stick pan. When the potatoes are nice and golden add them to the tofu in the pan with the olives. Stir fry for a couple of minutes and sprinkle the parsley on top before serving. Delizioso!

Tofu and Tomatoes Salad

Ingredients

200g of tofu
400g of cherry tomatoes
1 red onion sliced
Pitted black olives
10 leaves of basil
5 leaves of mint
Extra virgin olive oil
Tamari
1 lemon

Cut the tomatoes in two, mix them with the
basil, mint and red onion, all chopped and
dressed with olive oil and lemon juice.
In a non stick pan saute' the tofu cut in cubes
with some oil, until nice and crispy, add some
tamari and let cool for about 15 minutes.
Put all the ingredient together in a ball,
including the little sauce of the tofu, mix well
and enjoy!

Seitan and Dhal Hummus Wrap

Ingredients

1 wholemeal wrap
½ sliced small avocado
1 tablespoon of sliced red onion
70 gr of seitan cut in cubes or stripes
Dhal Hummus (p. 50)
Tamari

Pan fry the seitan cubes in a non stick pan, add a little dash of tamari and set aside. Take yout wrap and fill it with the hummus, avocado slices, red onion and seitan. Roll it, cut it in two and enjoy.

Nori Wrap with Em Wasabi Mayo

Ingredients

1 wholemeal wrap
1 sheet of toasted nori
Wasabi Em Mayo (p. 38)
100 gr of tofu cut in cubes or stripes
½ sliced small avocado
1 tablespoon of sliced red onion
Tamari

Pan fry the seitan cubes in a non stick pan, until golden brown on each side, add a little dash of tamari and set aside.
Place the nori on a plate and the wholemeal wrap on top. Fill the inside of the wholemeal wrap with the avocado slices, onion, tofu and Wasabi Em Mayo on top. Hold the nori and wrap together and roll them at the same time. If you have to much of nori at the side you can cut a little bit of the edges. Divide the wrap in two and ready!

Main Meals and Celebration Recipes

Adi Shakti, Adi Shakti, Adi Shakti, Namo Namo
Sarab Shakti, Sarab Shakti, Sarab Shakti,
Namo Namo
Pritham Bhagvati, Pritham Bhagvati, Pritham
Bhagvati, Namo Namo
Kundalini Mata Shakti, Mata Shakti, Namo
Namo, Shakti.
Shakti Mantra

Positive Thinking Quinoa Salad

Ingredients

200g quinoa
50g pine nuts
100g of dried soft apricots
1 medium red onion
400g sliced carrots
1 little bunch of parsley
10 leaves of mint
Extra virgin olive oil
Sea salt

Cook the quinoa as you would do with you steam rice, adding 1/2 teaspoon of salt to the water. Once it is ready pour it in a big bowl and put it on a side.
Cook the sliced carrots in the oven at 200 degrees with some olive oil, salt and pepper until they are all nice and golden brown. Let them cool down a little bit.
Cut the onion, the parsley and the mint very finely.
Cut the apricots in little pieces too.

Add the carrots*, the onion, parsley, mint, apricots and pine nuts to the quinoa and mix everything with a generous sparkling of olive oil, crumble the feta cheese on top and mix again. It is lovely both a little warm or cold. Perfect with any variation of hummus at the side. Perfect for film nights and cinematic travelling!

*Instead of carrots you can use roasted pumpkin cubes.

Middle February Quinoa Salad

Ingredients

250g of quinoa
1 bunch of spring onions
3 deseeded red chillies
1 little bunch of parsley
20 leaves of fresh mint
500g of pumpkin
200g of tofu
Extra virgin olive oil
Salt

Cook the quinoa as you'd normally cook your steam rice and leave it on the side.
Slice the pumpkin and dress it with olive oil, salt and pepper, put it in a non-stick tray and then in the oven until nice and golden. Let it rest on the side.
In a non stick pan saute' the tofu* cut in cubes with some oil, until nice and crispy, add some tamari and let cool for about 15 minutes.
Cut the spring onions, parsley, mint and chillies in small pieces.

Assemble all the ingredients in a big bowl, add some olive oil, mix everything together and taste to see if you need to add some salt or oil.

*Instead of the tofu you can olso use seitan or feta cheese. And again, a bit of hummus at the side works very well.

Millet Tabbouleh

Ingredients

250g of millet
70g of parsley
30g of mint leaves
500g of tomatoes
2 red onions
Extra virgin olive oil
Salt

Put the millet in a pan, cover with slightly salty water. The water should be about 3 cm above the millet. Bring to boil and cook at medium high heat for a minute. Mix the millet, bring the heat to the minimum and let cook with the lid on for about 15 minutes or until the water is completely dried and the millet is soft. Take the millet off the heat and let it cool down in a salad bowl.
Finely chop the parsley, mint and onions. Chop the tomatoes and add to the millet together with the parsley, mint, onion, a good dash of olive oil and salt to taste.

Millet Croccantina with Hot Chillie Beans

Ingredients for the Millet Croccantina

250g of millet
1 liter of water
Extra virgin olive oil
Salt

Put the millet in a pan, cover with a slightly salty litre of water. Bring to boil and cook at medium high heat for a minute. Mix the millet, bring the heat to the minimum and let cook with lid for about 15 minutes or until the water is completely dried and the millet is really soft. Take the millet off the heat dress with some oil of olive and mix well.
Put a bit of oil on a oven tray too and distribute the millet nicely on it, making like a cake of no more than 2 cm.
Dash with a little oil on the top and cook in pre heated oven at 200 degrees, until a lovely golden crust is formed at the bottom and top.

For the Hot Black Beans

400g of cooked black beans
1 can of chopped tomatoes
5 cloves of garlic
1 large onion
5 deseeded red chillies (if you like very hot leave the seeds in one of them)
Extra virgin olive oil
1 little bunch of parsley
1 teaspoon of organic granulated vegan stock
Salt to taste

Finely chop the onion, garlic and chillies and soute' them in a pan with 4 or 5 tablespoons of olive oil. When they start to golden add the tomatoes, the stock and a couple of tablespoons of water. Once the sauce starts to boil, lower the heat, cover with lid and let cook for about 30 minutes. If you see that the sauce dries to much add another couple of spoons of water. Add the beans and let cook for other 10 minutes. Take it off the heat and stir in the parsley finely chopped. Serve with the Millet Croccantina and if you like with some yogurt dip (p. 41) at the side.

Chickpeas Focaccia

This is a great recipe! It is a traditional Italian recipe from Tuscany but there is also another version from Liguria, totally Vegan! The result is a yummy kind of focaccia but so rich in protein. As a good matching veggie dish I chose saute cauliflower and some Kali's dip (p. 43)

Ingredients

200g chickpea flour
750ml water
Extra virgin olive oil
750ml water
Salt

Put the flour in the bowl and pour the water a little at a time, stirring carefully. Add salt, stir and let it sit in the bowl throughout the night. In the morning, remove with a slotted spoon the foam if it has formed on the surface, add the 3 tablespoons of oil and stir in until absorbed.

Preheat oven to 250 ° and heat a roasting tray, remove it being careful not to burn yourself. Grease it with a little oil and pour the liquid in it, the focaccia should be about 2 cm, don't be too precise.
Place the pan in the lower guide and cook for 45 minutes,
At the end it should remain soft (but not too soggy) and golden and almost crisp at the top, enjoy!

*You could try adding some spice and herbs like paprika, cumin or rosemary to the flour chickpeas mix before putting it in the tray.

Oltrecielo, New Moon/Solar Eclipse Spicy Cauliflower Pie

I own a magic place in the countryside near Pavia, which is a lovely old town near Milan, in Italy. It is indeed a beautiful place but the greatest thing about it are the people, friends around it. During a party celebration for an intense New Moon and Solar Eclipse day Andrea Balam and Lella Sujati, yoga instructor and owner of Oltrecielo a great yoga school in the neighbourhood, brought this magnificent Cauliflower Pie. I present it to you with a little variation, the added potatoes. You are going to love it!

Ingredients for the pastry

300g wholemeal wheat flour
120ml of water
1/2 teaspoon of salt
3 tablespoon of extra virgin olive oil
Yeast

For the filling

1 cauliflower
2 medium potatoes
1 onion
2 cloves of garlic
1 tablespoon of a good indian masala
Vegetable stock
Extra virgin olive oil and salt to taste

Combine water, salt, oil and yeast and add to the flour. Begin to knead, until dough is smooth and compact. Let it rest for at least an hour. In the mean time make the filling. Chop the potatoes in small cubes and put them aside. Chop onion and garlic finely and saute' them in a large pan. Add the cauliflower, stir well, add a glass of stock and cook until tender. Add the potatoes and the masala. Let cook for about 5 minutes, until the potatoes are cooked al dente and let cool aside.
Knead the dough for another 5 minutes and start to roll out it with the rolling pin to make a thin pastry.
Coat a round baking tin of about 25 cm, covered with baking paper, add the filling and cover with another sheet.

Bake in preheated oven at 200 degrees for about 25 minutes or until golden brown.

*Try adding some olives instead of the masala. Wait at least 20 minutes before cutting it. Otherwise it will be difficult to have nice and neat slices. Its lovely even cold for up to three days.

Em Burgers

Ingredients

450 gr of any pulses sprouts (lentils, beans, chickpeas you can even mix them)
3 tablespoons of your wholemeal flour
2 tablespoons of oat's flakes
½ teaspoon of baking soda
1/3 of teaspoon of cumin
½ teaspoon of salt
Extra virgin olive oil

In the mixer, blend the sprouts, baking soda, cumin and salt.
Transfer the mixture in a container and add the flour and the oat's flakes.
Leave in the fridge for at least 5 hours.
After the time required, place some baking paper on a baking tray and spread some olive oil on it. The mixture is not going to be very dry, so with the help of a spoon shape some burgers until you finish it. Put some olive oil on top of each and bake in preheated oven at about 200 degrees until your burgers are nice and golden brown.

Turn them a couple of times to really obtain a nice crust on each side.

You can enjoy them like this, with some salad at the side or you can really treat them like burgers. In this case, spread your favorite sauce on both side of an wholemeal bun (Em Ketchup, Em Mayo, Kali's Dip etc.), place your burger on top and finish with sliced red onion, a slice of tomato and a leaf of iceberg.

Tofu, "Aglio, Olio & Peperoncino" Rice Linguine

Ingredients

250 gr of wholemeal rice linguine (or other kind of wholemeal spaghetti)
200g of tofu
100g of baby spinach
7 cloves of garlic
3 chopped fresh red chillies, with or without seeds
Extra virgin oil of olive

In a pan with a dash of olive oil, crumble the tofu, add a little salt to taste and keep pan frying until the tofu is nice and golden.
Crush the garlic in a larger pan with some olive oil, add the chopped chillies and pan fry until the garlic starts to golden, but make sure to not brown. Turn the heat off and add the crumbled tofu to the garlic pan.
Start bringing to boil the water with a tablespoon of salt to cook the linguine. When

the salty water is boiling add the linguine and let them cook for the necessary time written on the packaging, usually it's between 11 and 12 minutes. A minute before draining the spaghetti add the spinach.

When the water starts to boil again drain everything.

Bring the tofu pan on the heat again, add the linguine and spinach, and stir fry for just few seconds.

Wholemeal Spaghetti with Beauty Spell Pesto

Ingredients

50g of watercress
50g of rocket
60g walnuts
40g almonds
3 small cloves of garlic
50ml extra virgin olive oil
350g wholemeal spaghetti
50g of grated goat cheese (optional)
Sea salt
Water

In a large pan start bringing to boil the water with a tablespoon of salt in which you will cook the spaghetti.
With the mixer blend the watercress with the garlic and the olive oil. 50ml of oil should be enough to be able to blend this ingredient and to obtain a creamy paste. If this is a bit too difficult add a couple of tablespoon of water and a little bit more olive oil.

Add the walnuts to the mixture and blend for few seconds more. Don't add any salt.
When the salty water is boiling add the spaghetti and let them cook for the necessary time written on the packaging, usually it's between 11 an 12 minutes. A minute before draining the spaghetti, take a bit of the cooking water from the pan and put it aside.
Drain the spaghetti and mix them with the creamy paste in a large bowl . Add a couple tablespoons of the water that was put aside and some grated goat cheese if you like and if it is your non totally vegan day. Mix well and buon appetito!

Spelt Pasta with Romanesco Broccoli and Seitan of the LaboratorioVeg

This is a super delicious recipe inspired by the LaboratorioVeg one. The LaboratorioVeg is an amazing vegan blog filled with inspiring recipes unfortunately still only in Italian. But lovely Samantha promised that the English version is on its way. Going back to our Romanesco Broccoli and Seitan pasta, this is seriously one of my favorite pasta dishes, enjoy!

Ingredients

300g of spelt spaghetti
400g of romanesco broccoli's florets
200g of seitan chopped in small cubes
2 tablespoons of bread crumbs
3 cloves of garlic
2 chillies with or without seeds
Extra virgin olive oil
Salt

Start heating some salted water in a pan to cook the pasta later.

In a large pan saute' chillies and crushed garlic. Once the garlic is nice and golden and is gifting you with that irresistible smell, add the seitan, let soute' for other 4 or 5 minutes and set aside.

In another little pan, fry the bread crumbs in a few tablespoons of olive oil and set aside.

When the water is boiling add the pasta. As soon as the water starts to boil again, wait a minute and add the broccoli's florets and let cook for the time required for the pasta. Drain the pasta with the florets, leaving less than 1/2 glass of the water they've been cooking in aside.

Bring the pan with the garlic and seitan on the heat again and stir in the pasta with the broccoli, stir fry just for a minute more adding a couple of tablespoons of their own water we put aside before.

Divide into plates and sprinkle the fried breadcrumbs on top. Buon Appetito!

Pumpkin, Olives and Seitan Penne

Ingredients

350g of wholemeal penne
500g of Pumpkin cut in cubes
250g of seitan cutter in cubes
olives
1 chilli with or without seeds
Extra virgin oil of olive
2 cloves of garlic
Salt

Use your hands to nicely dress the pumpkin on a baking tray with a little olive oil and roast it. Put the seitan in a bowl with two tablespoons of olives oil and one of tamari and set aside. Crush 2 cloves of garlic and quick fry them for a minute, being careful not to brown it. Add the seitan cubes, olives and stir fry until the seitan starts to brown.
Cook the pasta al dente in salty water and quickly put it in the olives, garlic and seitan pan. Add the pumpkin and stir fry on high heat for few seconds. Beautiful!

Em Ragu' Sauce with
Seitan and Porcini

Ingredients

250g of Seitan
2 cans of chopped tomatoes
3 tablespoons of tomato paste
1 onion finely chopped
1 clove of garlic crushed
100g of dried porcini
1 pinch of crushed chilli peppers
1 little bunch of fresh Basil
Extra virgin olive oil
Salt

Let the porcini soak in a cup of warm water
In a small non stick pan stir fry the seitan
chopped in cubes and put it aside. Saute'
onion and garlic until they are so soft you
could even mash them. Drain the porcini and
save their water. Add them to the onion and
garlic and soute' for another minute.
Add the tomato paste, stir for one minute and
then add the water of the porcini and the

chopped tomatoes, stir well and when it starts to boil let cook at low heat, with the lid on for about 1 hour.

After 1 hour take off the lid and let cook for another 15 minutes at medium heat. Add the seitan and let cook for other 5 minutes. Add all the basil and let flavoring off of the heat for about 15 minutes

The Ragu' is ready. Discard the basil and you can use it to dress any other kind of pasta, ravioli, gnocchi, risotto or polenta.

*A wise thing to do is to make a good quantity to save in portion container to defrost when you need a quick, healthy and delicious pasta meal.

Wholemeal Lasagne with Pumpkin and Walnuts Sauce

Ingredients

500g of wholemeal lasagne sheets
1kg of pumpkin
1litre of soy milk
5 tablespoons of plain flour
200g of walnuts
1 clove of garlic
Extra virgin olive oil
Salt
Pepper

Prepare the sauce by blending flour, soy milk, salt, pepper and two tablespoons of olive oil. Put it on the stove at low heat, stirring with a whisk to avoid lumps. Allow to simmer unti you have a smooth and thick consistency and let it cool.
Cook the lasagne sheets al dente in salty water and keep them aside.
Cut the pumpkin in little slices or cubes and roast it in the oven with olive oil and salt until

nice and soft.

To make the walnut sauce, blend the walnuts with few tablespoons of the milk sauce and the garlic clove.

Time to assemble the lasagne.

Take a tray of about 25x35cm. Put some oil at the bottom and a little of the milk sauce. Do the first layer of lasagne, distribute half of the pumpkin on top, little teaspoons all over the pumpkin of walnuts sauce and some teaspoons of milk sauce to finish. Cover with another lasagne sheet layer and adjust pumpkin, walnut sauce and milk sauce as before. Do another lasagne sheet layer and top up just with the rest of the milk sauce and little teaspoon drops of walnuts sauce.

Cook in preheated oven at 200 degrees for about 40 minutes or until nice and golden on the top. Don't let it stay too much in the oven anyway or it will dry too much. Let it rest out of the oven for about ten minutes before cutting to serve.

Pasta with Courgettes

Ingredients

350g of wholemeal pasta
70 gr of pine nuts
500 gr of sliced courgettes
3 garlic cloves
1 little bunch of basil
Extra virgin olive oil

Use your hands to nicely dress the courgettes
on a baking tray with a little of olive oil and
cook them in the oven at about 210 degrees
until golden.
Crush the garlic and quick fry it for a minute,
being careful not to brown it. Add the pine nuts
and stir for few seconds.
Cook the pasta aldente in salty water, drain it
and quickly put it in the garlic and pine nuts
pan. Add the courgettes and stir fry on high
heat for few seconds. Sprinkle with chopped
basil and serve immediately.

Creamy Curry with
Pan Fried Koyadofu Cakes

For the Curry

Ingredients

1 can of chopped tomatoes
1 small/medium carrot
2 medium onions
1 piece of ginger (about 1x1 cm)
1 clove of garlic
1 red hot chilli with or without seeds
2 tablespoons of dry coconut flakes
2 tablespoons of good quality organic smooth peanut butter
1 glass of water
1/2 teaspoon of granulated organic vegetarian stock
2 tablespoons of white miso or more to taste

Put tomatoes, the chilli, onions and carrot roughly chopped, coconut flakes, granulated stock and the glass of water in a pan and bring to boil. Cover with lid and let it cook until the

vegetables are all nice and soft.
Let cool down for about 20 minutes. Add garlic and ginger and blend until nice and smooth. Warm up again and just when it is about to boil again take off from the heat and stir in the peanuts butter and miso.

For the Koyadofu cakes

Ingredients

4 Koyadofu cakes
500ml of water for soaking
500ml of water for the stock
1 teaspoon of organic vegetarian granulated stock
2 sheets of kombu
3 tablespoons of Tamari
Sunflower oil

While you are waiting for the curry to cook, make the Koyadofu cakes.
Soak the Koyadofu cakes in 500ml of water for about 10 minutes.
In the mean time prepare the stock adding to the other 500ml of water the tsp of granulated stock, the kombu sheets, and tamari and bring

to boil.

Squeeze gently the Koyadofu cakes to remove excess moisture and add them to the boiling kombu stock and cook for about 7 minutes. Turn off the heat and let sit for other 7 minutes. Remove them from the liquid and squeeze the liquid.

Heat the oil in a frying pan and add the Koyadofu cakes.

Let them fry until golden brown to each side.

Assemble the dish

Serve each Koyadofu on a plate with some steam rice, the curry on top and some steam green vegetables at the side I usually have fine beans.

Chickpeas Tagine

Ingredients

750g of red peppers (or red and yellow)
250g of potatoes
450g of cooked chickpeas
2 onions
3 cloves of garlic
180g of pitted kalamata olives
1 can of chopped tomatoes
2 red chillies
2 teaspoons of granulated stock
4 teaspoons of paprika
½ teaspoon of cumin
700ml of hot water
Extra virgin olive oil

Slice the onions, crush the garlic, chop the chillies and saute' in 7 tablespoons of olive oil, until soft and start to golden. Add the peppers cut in square pieces and sauté at high heat for a minute. Add the potatoes cut in cubes, chickpeas, olives, granulated stock, paprika and cumin, mix well and add the tomatoes, mix again and stir in the 700ml of water. Let everything cook slowly with lid, until the vegetables are soft. Make sure you are not overcooking the potatoes, they have to stay firm and don't mash in the sauce.

Once your Tagine is ready the best way to enjoy it would be to let it rest one hour to cool down and then ½ a day in the fridge and then warm it up before eating. In this way it really brings out all the flavors and the right consistency. And it is also very handy for a dinner party because you can make it in advance. In any case it is really good even if you want to eat it straight away.

Serve with couscous.

Seitan with Creamy Chickpeas Sauce of the LaboratorioVeg

Ingredients

500g of thin seitan steaks (you can use a whole seitan roast and slice it yourself)
300g of cooked chickpeas
1 tablespoon of tahini
The juce of 1 lemon
1 teaspoon of djon mustard
3 tablespoons of Em Mayo
10-15 small capers (optional but they really work)
1/2 teaspoon of paprika
1/2 teaspoon of cumin
Finaly chopped fresh parsley
Salt
Extra virgin olive oil

Thin slice the seitan and saute' in a pan with 2 tablespoons of extra virgin olive oil for about 2 minutes.
Prepare a sauce with the cooked chickpeas, the tahini, the mustard, capers, lemon juice,

paprika, cumin, 1 tablespoon of olive oil and salt to taste (don t make it too savory because you still have to add the mayo). Add enough water so that it appears like hummus consistency. Stir inn the mayo. You now have a tasty and creamy sauce to pour over the seitan, nicely sliced and arranged on a dish. Sprinkle with parsley singing Dancing Queen and serve.

Seitan with Onions

Ingredients

300g of seitan
7 medium onions
Extra virgin olive oil
Pepper
Tamari

Marinade the seitan cut in cubes in a little olive oil.
Slice the onions finely. Saute' them in 4-5 tablespoons of olive oil until they are very soft and golden. Add the seitan and stir fry for other 5 minutes. Sprinkle some tamari and serve with steam rice, a good quality toasted country bread or even roast potatoes.

Roast Potatoes or Pumpkin with Seitan

Ingredients

300g of seitan
750g of potatoes or pumpkin
Rosemary
Extra virgin olive oil
Salt

Cut the Seitan in cubes, marinate with tamari,
a few tablespoons of olive oil, some rosemary
and let it rest on the side.
Meanwhile prepare the potatoes or pumpkin.
Cut them in cubes and put them on a tray. Mix
them well with olive oil and salt and put in a
preheated oven at 200 degrees.
When they are almost ready and becoming the
roast potatoes of your dreams add the
marinated seitan, include the rosemary and stir
well. Let roast for just other 5 minutes and
serve with your favorite dip.

Lemon Soy Scaloppine

Ingredients

250g of dehydrated soya chunks
Plain organic flour
The juice of two lemons
Extra virgin olive oil
1 litre of vegetables stock
1 piece of kombu of about 10 cm
Tamari

Heat the stock and when it starts to boil add Kombu and soy chunks. Let them cook for about 20 minutes or read the time required on the packaging. When they are nice and soft, drain them and let them cool. Dust them with about 2-3 tablespoons of flour and mix well. Heat 7 tablespoons of olive oil in a large non stick pan and saute' the soy chuncks until they start browing all around. Add the lemon juice, mix well and before serving add a couple of tablespoons of Tamari. You are going to love them! Try with basmati rice and stir fry courgettes at the side.

Em Polenta

Ingredients

250g of chickpeas flour
250g of Italian style cornmeal for polenta, fine
or course
2 teaspoons of salt
2 litres of water

In a high edges pan, dissolve both the two
flours and salt in the 2 litres of water. Bring to
boil and keep cooking at very low heat and
always stirring, for about 30/40 minutes.
Once your Em Polenta is ready you can serve
it immediately, maybe with some Em Ragu' (p.
96) on top or with hot beans (p. 81) or any
other side vegetable dish of your choice.
If you have left over, once it rests in the fridge
you can slice it and fry the slices in hot oil,
really nice!

Quinoa Gnocchi with Radicchio and Walnuts Sauce

Ingredients

150g of quinoa flour
100g of wholemeal spelt flour
400 gr of radicchio
100g of walnuts
200ml of soy cream
1 clove of garlic
Extra virgin olive oil
1/3 teaspoon of paprika
Water
Pepper
Salt

Mix together the two flours with 200ml of warm water and a pinch of salt. Make a smooth dough, cover with a film and let rest for 30 minutes. In the mean time, slice the radicchio and saute in a little olive oil and a little salt until the water that brings out evaporates and it softens. Let saute' another minute and put to the side.
Make the walnut sauce blending the walnuts

with the garlic, soy cream, paprika, pepper and salt to taste in the mixer. Make a nice smooth cream, if it's too tick just add one or two tablespoons of soy milk or simply water.

With the dough make the gnocchi shape kind of snakes/tubes, then cut them in sections of about 1 cm.

Bring a pan with salty water to boil and cook the gnocchi until soft, it should be for about 15 minutes. But taste them, because it will also depends on the quality of the flours.

Bring the pan with the radicchio on the heat again and add the drained gnocchi. Mix well and take off from the heat. Stir in the walnut sauce and serve hot.

"In mythos and fairy tales, deities and other great spirits test the hearts of humans by showing up in various forms that disguise their divinity. They show up in robes, rags, silver sashes, or with muddy feet. They show up with skin dark as old wood, or in scales made of rose petal, as a frail child, as a lime-yellow old woman, as a man who cannot speak, or as an animal who can. The great powers are testing to see if humans have yet learned to recognize the greatness of soul in all its varying forms."

Clarissa Pinkola Estés, Women Who Run With the Wolves: Myths and Stories of the Wild Woman Archetype

Sweet Comforts and Raw Treats

*"We are made of the same stuff that dreams
are made of "*
William Shakespeare

Dates Truffles

Ingredients

150g of dried pitted soft dates
50g of whole almonds flour (possibly
Homemade, easy done putting for few
seconds the almonds in the mixer)
50g of almonds flour to dust the truffles at the
end
The zest of 1 lemon
Water

Blend the dates with the lemon zest and a
couple of tablespoons of water, or enough
water to be able to blend the dates in a thick
puree.
Add 50g of almond flour and let the mixture
rest in the fridge for a couple of hours.
After two hours, make little balls with the dates
and almond paste and roll them in the rest of
the almond flour and keep them in the fridge
for readymade, lovely raw treats.

Chocolate Truffles

Ingredients

150g dates
50g of walnuts or hazelnuts
1 tablespoon of cocoa powder + some to dust
the truffle at the end
100g of good quality 70% chocolate

Blend the nuts that you choose in the mixer
until powdered.
Blend the dates with a couple of tablespoons
of water, or enough water to be able to blend
the dates in a tick purée. Melt the chocolate in
the microwave and mix everything nicely
together, nuts flour, chocolate, the tablespoon
of cocoa powder and the dates puree (if you
fancy something different you can even add
some orange zest or a pinch of chili powder).
Refrigerate for at least two hours. After the
time required make little balls with the mixture
and dust them in the rest of cocoa powder and
keep them refrigerated until the moment you
need to treat yourself or someone special.

Kerala Dreamin' Raw Carrots Truffles

Ingredients

250g of pitted dates
100g of almond flour
200g of finely grated carrots
3 cardamom cloves
150ml water
1 tablespoon of rose water
50g of oat flakes
100g of coconut flakes
The juice of 1 lemon
1 tablespoon of agave syrup
More coconut flakes to dust the truffles

Blend the oat until like flour.
Put all the ingredients, together with the oat flour, in the mixer adding the 150ml of water, little by little.
The mixture has to rest in the fridge for about eight hours, so make sure you make it in the morning for the evening and in the evening for the morning.
After the required time, make truffles balls and

dust them in some coconut flakes.
Keep them in the fridge and eat within a week.

*Instead of the lemon juice you can try with the juice and zest of ½ orange.

Istant Bluberry Ice cream

Ingredients

250g of frozen blueberries
7 tablespoons of milk kefir
2 tablespoons of agave syrup

Blend all the ingredients in the mixer, divided in nice ice cream cups or in cones and enjoy immediately.

*You can really use different kinds of berries and fruits like strawberries, mango, etc.

Em Nutella

Ingredients

170g of hazelnut butter
70g of soy cream
70g of agave syrup
3 teaspoons of cocoa powder

Warm up the hazelnuts cream just a little
bit, usually when you open the jar it's a little
too hard. Add the agave and mix well. Add the
cocoa powder and mix well. Stir in the soy
cream and mix well until smooth, gorgeous
and very decadent! Put it in a glass jar and eat
it in 5 days. I'm sure it will last much less.

Em Shortbread Pastry

Ingredients

400g of wholemeal flour
100g of almond flour
150ml of good quality oil
170g of fructose
The zest of 1 lemon
1 tablespoon of soy milk if needed

Mix the two flours nicely together. Add all the other ingredients except the milk. Roughly and quickly mix everything, for a very little time. If the dough is to dry add just one or two tablespoons of soy milk.
Make a ball and refrigerate for about two hours.
Use it to make tarts of every kind, using your hands to roll it out.

Em Apple Pie

Ingredients

300g of Spelt flour
150g of almond flour
1/2 teaspoon of baking soda
The zest of 1 lemon
1/2 teaspoon of cinnamon
250g of fructose
700g of apple finely sliced
100ml of organic soy, corn or peanuts oil
More agave syrup for the tray layer
Soy milk

Mix well together the two flours, sugar, oil,
zest, cinnamon, baking soda.
Grease a non stick cake tray (about 21 cm
diameter) and spread the bottom with a layer
of agave syrup.
Add the sliced apples to the flour mixture and
nicely mix them together. It will seem that
there are too many apples for the mixture, no
there are not, they' re just perfect! Carefully put
everything in the tray on top of the agave

syrup layer. Cook in preheated oven at 180 degrees for about 1 hour. When it is cooked, let it rest until completely cold before cutting.

Chocolate Orange Cake

Ingredients

1 whole orange
150g of fructose
100g of 70% dark chocolate, melted
1 full tablespoon of cocoa powder
150g of almonds flour
200g of plain flour
100ml almond milk
½ teaspoon of baking soda

For the icing
150g 70% dark chocolate, melted
3 tablespoons agave syrup

Put the orange in a pan with 350ml of water, cover and cook until soft. Leave to cool, still covered.
Heat the oven to 180 degrees. Line a 20cm

round tin with baking paper.

Cut the orange in half and remove the pips. Put in the mixer with 5 tablespoons of the orangey liquid left in the pan and blitz to a smooth puree, scraping down the bowl a couple of times. Melt the chocolate in a little pan at very low heat. In the mixer add the fructose, melted chocolate, cocoa powder, almonds flour, almond milk, flour and baking powder to the orange puree and whizz again to mix thoroughly.

Bake for 50 minutes, in a tin using some eco roasting paper underneath. Cool in the tin. To make the icing, melt the rest of the chocolate. It will start to seize so mix in the agave syrup and it will go shiny again. Transfer the cake onto a plate or stand then simply ice the top and all around.

Lemon Honey Cake

Ingredients

200g of almonds flour
150g of wheat flour
350g of honey
50g of fructose
100ml of almond milk
2 tablespoons of sunflowers oil or coconut butter
1/2 teaspoon of baking soda
The zest of 2 lemons
The juice of 2 lemons
1 tablespoon of agave syrup

Combine flour, almond flour, honey, fructose, almond milk, oil, baking soda and the zest of the lemons. Mix well until nice and smooth. Grease a baking tin, fill it up with the mixture and bake for about 30 minutes, in preheated oven at 180 degrees. Add the agave syrup to the lemon juice and when the cake is cooked turn it upside down and pour over the lemons and agave syrup liquid. Let cool down for at least 30 minutes before serving.

Before Bed Tips

Wait at least three hours after dinner before going to bed.
A nice and relaxing herbal tea is a warm and loving gesture to prepare yourself entering the dream's kingdom with all the time, peace and kindness your heart needs to let go, rest and welcome oneiric gifts.
Another healthy and more nutritious goodnight drink is the Golden Milk. You can prepare it simmering 1/4 of teaspoon of turmeric with ½ cup of water on a low heat, until you have a nice paste. Bring to boil 250 ml of your favorite milk with a cardamom pod. Remove from heat, remove the cardamom pod and add raw honey to taste.

"Shake the hand that feeds you."

Michael Pollan
In Defense of Food: An Eater's Manifesto

Bibliography

Osho. Creativity: Unleashing the Forces Within. St Martin's Press, 2000

Isabel Allende. Aphrodite. Harper Perennial, 1999

Clarissa Pinkola Estés, Women Who Run With the Wolves. Rider, 1992

Georges Ohsawa. La Dieta Macrobiotica. Astrolabio-Ubaldini Editore s.r.l, 1968

Michio Kushi. Macrobiotica. red edizioni, 2003

Mari Fujii. The Enlightened Kitchen.Kodansha International Ltd, 2005

Mayumi Nishimura. Mayumi's Kitchen.Kodansha International Ltd, 2010

Michael Pollan. The Omnivore's Dilemma. The Penguin Press, 2006

Michael Pollan. In Defense of Food: An Eater's Manifesto. Penguin Book, 2009

Michael Pollan. Cooked. Penguin Books, 2013

Emma Graf. La Cucina a Base di Cereali. Natura e Cultura Editrice, 2009

The Sivananda Yoga Vedanta Centers. The Yoga Cookbook. Gaia Books Limited, 1999

Jessica Porter. The Hip Chick's Guide to Macrobiotics. Penguin Group, 2004

Julia Ponsonby and Schumacher College. Gaia's Kitchen. Green Books, 2008

T. Colin Campbell and Thomas M. Campbell. The China Study. BenBella Books, Inc, 2006.

William Dufty. Sugar Blues. Time Warner International; Warner Books Ed edition, 2002

Documentaries

Food Inc. 2010 by Robert Kenner
Jamie Oliver's Food Revolution 2010-2011 by
Jamie Oliver
Jamie's School Dinners 2005 with Jamie Oliver
by Guy Gilbert
SuperSizeMe 2004 by Morgan Spurlock
Jamie's Kitchen 2002-Return to Jamie's
Kitchen 2003 with Jamie Oliver, Channel 4

Web Sites

http://www.macrobiotics.co.uk
http://vandanashiva.com
https://www.biodynamics.com
http://www.biodynamic.org.uk
http://www.biodinamica.org
http://www.kushiinstitute.org
http://www.laboratorioveg.it
http://www.theppk.com
http://www.clearspring.co.uk
http://www.slowfood.com
http://tablehurst.farm
http://www.tablehurstandplawhatch.co.uk/P
lawhatch.html
http://carolyncowan.com
http://www.wholefoodsmarket.com
http://www.oltrecielo.it
http://www.cascineorsine.it
http://www.march-against-monsanto.com
http://www.infinityfoodswholesale.co.uk
http://www.laterraeilcielo.it
http://www.kombuchakamp.com
http://www.equinoxkombucha.com
http://www.teapigs.co.uk
https://www.yogiproducts.com